'Merry Christmas,
Jessica & Joey Lee
Mary Cooper Smith .
cathy smith

A Day in the Life of

William Bray Goat

The tale of a frisky pygmy goat and his visit to the stable.

Illustrations by Mary Cooper Smith
Text by Cathy Smith

A Day in the Life of Wiliam Bray Goat
©1999 by Mary Cooper Smith, artist, and Cathy Smith, author
ISBN 1-889668-11-7

William Bray Goat really did exist. We met him at Bray's Island Plantation, located outside of Beaufort, South Carolina. He was a young pygmy goat who belonged to the riding instructor.

William Bray Goat and Bray's Island are named for William Bray, an Indian trader who worked among the Yemassee Indians in the early eighteenth century. The land in the vicinity of the current Bray's Island belonged to him until he died in April, 1715, during the Yemassee War. Bray's family sold the land about 18 years after his death.

Although several skirmishes erupted there during the Revolutionary War, the property and surrounding plantations were considered "no man's land" during the Civil War and were occupied by neither Confederate nor Federal troops.

To young adventurers everywhere.

William Bray Goat stands on a pillow on the front seat of the red farm truck.
William is a baby pygmy goat and very short.
He can barely see out of the window without his pillow.

He will soon be on his way to the stable with Julie and her mother.

After they arrive at the stable, William wriggles down from Julie's arms.

His eyes sparkle and he goat-grins.

Wow!

What wonderful new places and sights and smells!

William scampers about in his funny, wobbly gait.

He wobbles into a barn with hay in the stalls…

soft to roll in, but better to eat!

Outside, William finds that the horses are friendly to visit...

but a tractor is more fun to climb up on!

William strolls away, then stops and turns quickly at a buzzing sound.

He feels a soft flutter around his tail… but nothing is there.

He skips once and scratches at a sudden tickle on his front hoof. Hmmm... still nothing.

Then he swats at a buzzing sound in his right ear. He frowns and wrinkles his brow.

Then — WHOA! Right in front of him is a huge, black horsefly! It looks as big as his head!

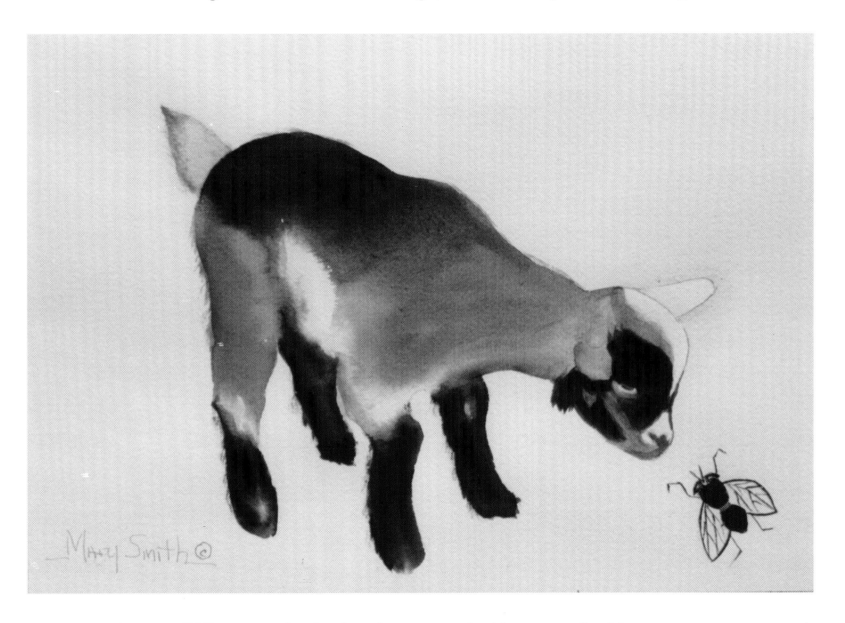

The horsefly eyes William, circles his head twice, and with a great final b-z-z-z-z-z, zooms away!

William throws back his head and bleats with baby goat laughter!

William wanders around to the front of the barn, and spies a flowering bush near the door.

Tired from all his activity, he nestles down and munches
on the tender leaves of a trailing branch until...

Spike, a yappy Jack Russell terrier, dashes past. William leaps to his feet, eager to play. Spike darts back and forth between William's dancing legs.

Too soon, though, a whistle sends the terrier scurrying off after one of the stable hands.

William isn't alone for long. He spots the barn cat, Lucy, sunning near the barn door. Even better, he sees a little grain on the ground nearby. He walks right past Lucy and licks up the grain.

Good stuff! Maybe there's a little more, so William sniffs around the entrance to the barn.

Uh-oh! What's that sound? William turns his ear to a corner of the barn and, yes, he hears a gnawing sound!

He moves forward cautiously and — hey there! A MONSTROUS MOUSE chews furiously on a corn cob. The mouse is as big - bigger! - than the corn cob!

His eyes glow red in the shadows. He blinks once. Twice. Then he inches closer to William in quick, jerky mouse-steps.

William's eyes widen and his knees begin to shake. He swallows hard.

William feels sure the hungry mouse does not want to be friends! Terrified, he dashes out of the barn as fast as his wobbly legs allow.

Once safely outside, William hears a sound that he knows right away.

G-r-r-r-rumble... his stomach reminds him that it is time for another snack.

Hey, why not share with his new friend, Sam?

Then William finds his favorite snack in a small room in the stable office: a whole roll of mysterious, flimsy white paper! Boy, is it tasty (even if it does stick to his teeth)!

Julie's mom doesn't agree, and shoos him away.

At last William's stomach is quiet. His eyes droop. He curls up on a horse blanket… and naps…

until Julie comes to carry him back to the truck.
William closes his eyes again, smiles sleepily

and dreams about his busy, happy day at the stable — and tomorrow…

The End

Though she has published nonfiction and humor pieces, this is Cathy Smith's first picture book. She holds her M.A. in English from Marshall University and has been a writing instructor at the University of Kentucky in Lexington. She has been a member of the Society of Children's Book Writers and Illustrators, and is currently at work on a series of poems for children. Smith lives in Versailles, Kentucky.

Artist Mary Cooper Smith, a native of Rome, Georgia, is a former director of the Georgia Watercolor Society and has had over 40 one-person exhibitions. In 1993, she was chosen as "Artist of the Year" by the Rome Area Council for the Arts. Her first book of watercolor paintings, "Flowers of the South," was published in 1996.